Space Race

David Glover

Is there anyone out there?

Now, that's a question! Fifty years ago, no one had ever left planet Earth. Then, suddenly – **BOOM!** – men, women and animals blasted off into space! The race was on, to be the first to walk on the surface of the Moon. As this book is being written, robot space probes are searching for life on our neighbouring planet Mars. What will happen in your lifetime?

★ Will astronauts leave Earth to travel to Mars … and beyond?

★ Will people ever live in space? How will they survive? What will they discover?

★ Are there alien creatures out there, waiting to greet visitors from Earth with a friendly wave of their tentacles?

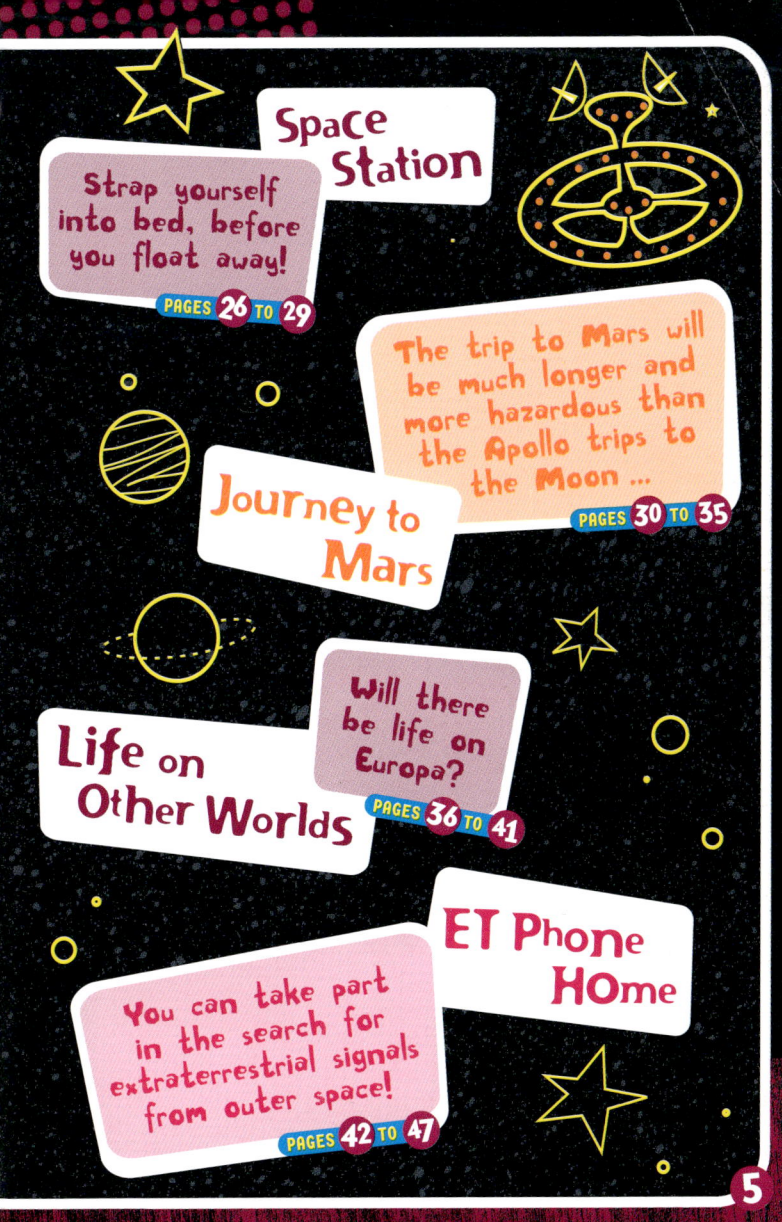

Space Station

Strap yourself into bed, before you float away!

PAGES 26 TO 29

Journey to Mars

The trip to Mars will be much longer and more hazardous than the Apollo trips to the Moon...

PAGES 30 TO 35

Life on Other Worlds

Will there be life on Europa?

PAGES 36 TO 41

ET Phone Home

You can take part in the search for extraterrestrial signals from outer space!

PAGES 42 TO 47

The Space Race

The space age began in October 1957, when the Russian satellite, Sputnik I, was launched into space. Sputnik was the first satellite to send signals back to Earth, but it was only the size of a **basketball!** Then, just one month later, a small dog called Laika (which means 'barker' in Russian) became the first living thing to travel into space. Laika was a passenger on Sputnik II. Though sadly Laika did not return to Earth, her journey helped to prove that human space flight would be possible. The launch of the Sputnik satellites started a 'space race' between Russia and America in the 1960s.

FuRRY FaCT

In August 1960, two more Russian dogs, Strelka and Belka, were sent into space on board Sputnik V ... and survived! They were the first animals to survive an orbital spaceflight!

Although Laika did not survive her space journey, two more dogs were sent into space in 1960.

Name
Yuri Gagarin

Nationality
Russian

Occupation
Worked in an iron works before joining the air force!

Life in space
First human being in space

On 12 April 1961, the Russian cosmonaut Yuri Gagarin won the race to be the first human being in space. Gagarin's space capsule orbited Earth just once, before plunging back through the atmosphere. For safety, Yuri Gagarin ejected from the capsule and parachuted to the ground before touchdown.

His whole flight lasted just 1 hour and 48 minutes (about the length of a football match), and he never went into space again. As the first man in space, Yuri Gagarin became a global superstar overnight. Sadly, Yuri died in 1968, when the jet fighter he was testing crashed near Moscow.

The Russian space capsule, Vostok I, successfully carried the first human being into space. Russia 1: America 0.

Mercury was a metal cone, just two metres tall by less than two metres wide – smaller than a family car!

The Americans may have been one down, but they were not far behind the Russians! On 5 May 1961, Alan Shepard was the first American to make a space flight. Unlike Gagarin, he did not orbit Earth. But his rocket reached a height of more than 100 miles (20 times higher than Mount Everest), before his capsule detached and parachuted back to the ground. This was not to be Shepard's only space flight. In 1971, he became just the fifth person to walk on the Moon.

What a Scorcher!

Shepard made his first journey into space inside a tiny metal capsule, called Mercury. Its thin metal skin had to protect him from temperatures as high as 3000°C as the capsule plunged back through the atmosphere at the end of the mission.

Conditions in space are very different to those on Earth. In space there is no air, your body feels weightless and the temperature can change from hot enough to cook you, to cold enough to freeze you, in seconds! For these reasons, the first astronauts in space spent their entire flight in space suits.

If an astronaut stepped outside a spacecraft without a spacesuit, they would die instantly! Their blood would boil, their eyes would burst and their body parts would explode!

FLoaTiNG FaCT

In 1965, Aleksei Leonov made the first space walk. He left his spacecraft and floated in space for ten minutes. After his walk he couldn't get back through the hatch because the air pressure in his suit had made the suit too stiff. He only managed to survive by letting some air out!

A space suit is airtight with its own oxygen supply. Water pipes run through the astronaut's underwear to control their body temperature. But how do you go to the toilet when you're wearing a space suit? You have to wear a special nappy! It must get very uncomfortable (and very **whiffy**) after a few days!

Valentina was first picked to become a cosmonaut because of her skill in parachute jumping!

During the 1960s, space exploration developed rapidly. From flights of a few hours, astronauts began to spend days and even weeks at a time in orbit. The first woman in space was Valentina Tereshkova. She flew aboard Vostok VI on 16th June 1963, and orbited Earth 48 times in her three day mission.

QUIZ A small dog called ***** was the first spac

As the space race quickened pace, the spacecrafts also developed rapidly. The American Mercury capsules were replaced by the bigger two-man Gemini spacecraft. On the Gemini III mission, astronaut Gus Grissom became the first person to eat a sandwich in space: he'd smuggled a corned beef sandwich inside his suit! He received a good telling off by ground control because weightless crumbs floated into important equipment!

> All this action was building towards the longest journey human beings have ever made – the journey to the Moon!

The Moon and Back

Since ancient times people have been fascinated by the Moon. How far away is it? What is it made from? Does anyone live there? Some people even believed that the Moon was made of green cheese! In 1865, Jules Verne wrote a story of a Moon expedition. He based his adventure on proper scientific calculations. It was so accurate that when the Apollo missions to the Moon were planned, NASA scientists were amazed by his predictions …

FiCTioN FaCT

The first science fiction book about space travel was published in 1638. It told the story of Domingo Gonzales who flew to the Moon in a chariot pulled by trained geese.

The Saturn V Rocket's engines produced as much force as 30 jumbo jets!

In Verne's book, three men take four days to travel to the Moon in an aluminium capsule weighing nine tons. In July 1969, the Apollo 11 took three men to the Moon in an aluminium craft weighing twelve tons. Their journey time was just over three days. The only main difference between Verne's story and the real Moon expedition was that Verne's capsule was fired by a giant gun, while the Apollo missions were launched by the giant Saturn V Rocket.

On 20 July 1969, the Lunar Lander 'Eagle' touched down on the Moon's surface. The Apollo 11 mission had safely landed the first man on the Moon! Neil Armstrong stepped down to the surface with the immortal words …

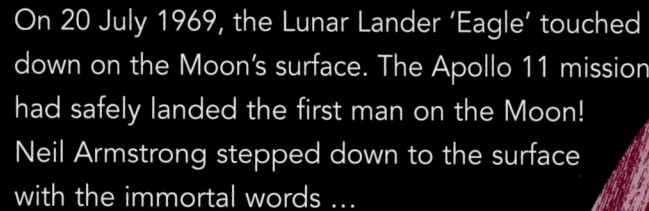

Neil Armstrong became the first human to stand on the Moon when he stepped out left foot first.

That's one small step for man – one **giant** leap *forward* for mankind.

In the three years from 1969 to 1972, there were six successful Apollo Moon landings. Life on board the Apollo space craft was more comfortable than in earlier space missions. The astronauts could take off their space suits and relax. They ate dried foods with choices such as beef and vegetables, and chocolate pudding on the menu. To eat the food, the astronaut added hot or cold water to the plastic pack, then squeezed the mixture through a nozzle into their mouth.

The Apollo 13 mission nearly ended in disaster. On day two of the flight, a faulty oxygen tank exploded. This threatened the astronauts with only three hours to stay alive! The story about how the three astronauts only just made it back to Earth has been told in a Hollywood film staring Tom Hanks as mission commander Jim Lovell.

Have you ever dropped a feather? It floats down slowly through the air. But on the Moon there is no air, so a feather falls as fast as a heavy hammer. The astronauts filmed the hammer and feather experiment on the Moon to prove that this is true.

22 QUIZ The ****** 13 mission nearly ended i

Survival on the Moon itself was not easy for the Apollo astronauts. There is no air on the Moon, so astronauts had to wear their space suits whenever they were outside the spacecraft. On Earth, the suits weigh 80 kilograms – as much as an astronaut's body. But luckily the Moon's gravity is just one sixth as strong as Earth's, so the suits did not seem so heavy.

The Apollo 15, 16 and 17 astronauts explored the Moon's surface in the Lunar Rover or 'Moon Buggy'. The astronauts collected samples of moon rock to bring back to Earth.

One Small Step...

Everyone remembers that Neil Armstrong was the first man to make his mark on the Moon, but what about the last man? Eugene Cernan was the last man to walk on the moon, and amazingly his footprints in the lunar dust will still be on the Moon today! Why? Well, there is no wind or water on the Moon, to blow or wash them away!

Space Station

It is now more than 30 years since the last Apollo mission to the Moon, but rockets are still blasting astronauts into Earth's orbit. These astronauts go to work onboard the International Space Station (ISS). The ISS has been built in space like a construction kit model. Its parts were delivered into orbit by both American and Russian space craft – working together, rather than racing against one another! The ISS is permanently manned by a crew of two people, who spend six months onboard. Other astronauts and scientists visit for days or weeks at a time.

FLuSH FaCT

At last! There are even proper toilets on the International Space Station. A suction system, with different shaped seats for men and women, makes sure nothing floats away!

The International Space Station is 73 metres long by 43 metres wide – almost the size of a football pitch!

Life on the ISS is much more comfortable than in the first space capsules. Inside, there is as much space as a large house, with several different rooms. There is more choice of food, exercise equipment and books and videos for entertainment. Here is what space shuttle pilot, Pamela Melroy, had for lunch during her tenth day in space.

Lunch onboard the ISS

Chicken strips in salsa
Thermostabilised

Macaroni and cheese
Rehydratable

Rice with butter
Thermostabilised

Macadamia nuts
Natural Form

Apple cider
Beverage

One big difference between living in space and on Earth is that in orbit you are weightless. You need to strap yourself into bed at night so you don't float away. Tidiness is very important too – imagine what your room would look like if all the things on the floor and shelves started to float about!

Journey to Mars

Blast off to the red planet! The next great challenge for humans in space is the journey to Mars. There are plans to make this trip in your lifetime, so you could be one of the astronauts on board! Mars is the fourth planet away from the Sun – check out the solar system on pages 36 to 37.

Mars is smaller and colder than Earth, and its atmosphere is very thin, having no oxygen. The temperature on the surface of Mars is, on average, about −60°C, so you will need to wrap up warm if you are planning a visit! Today, Mars is dry and barren, but valleys and gorges on its surface show that once rain fell, and there were rivers and oceans of liquid water. There is still ice frozen at the poles, and there may be liquid water under the Martian surface. Believe it or not, of all the other planets in our solar system, Mars is the most like Earth!

Robot space probes such as 'Spirit' and 'Opportunity' are searching for signs of life on the surface of Mars as this book is being written. But what exactly are they looking for? We already know there are no aliens waiting to jump out from behind rocks, but there could be evidence of life in the past on Mars.

FaCe FaCT

Mars is well-known for 'The Face', a hill in its northern plains. What is so special about this hill? Well, from above it looks like an extraterrestrial face!

Fossils or chemical deposits made by living things (like the chalk, oil and coal on Earth) could tell us whether Martian life has ever existed. Perhaps millions of years ago, when Mars was wet and warm, its oceans teamed with life like the oceans of Earth today.

> Space probes will be able to tell us if there are microscopic living things (like bacteria) still living beneath the Martian surface, in the ice and water deposits trapped there.

When the time comes, the trip to Mars will be much longer and more hazardous than the Apollo trips to the Moon. An expedition will last at least **two years**, with a journey time of about six months each way. To make the trip worthwhile, the astronauts will spend a year exploring the surface, living in a specially designed habitat. Inside their habitat, the Mars explorers will grow plants to provide food and to help keep their air fresh. They cannot rely on finding water, so they will recycle the water they take with them. At the end of a year, every drop they drink will have passed through everyone's bodies many times!

GET ME OUT OF HERE!

QUIZ An ********** to Mars will la

One of the main challenges for the Mars crew will be getting on with each other for all that time! They will be crammed together in a small space, six months away from home ... Imagine being locked in the Big Brother house for two years, with no possibility of being evicted!

PLUTO

NEPTUNE

URANUS

SATURN

JUPITER

Could there be life anywhere else in our **solar system**? There are nine planets altogether: Mercury, Venus, Earth, Mars, Jupiter, Saturn, Uranus, Neptune and Pluto. Most of the planets have moons. Perhaps we should be looking to these to find our nearest neighbours?

Venus was named after the goddess of love and beauty, probably because it is very bright compared to other planets.

Unfortunately, most places in the solar system are either much too hot or much too cold for life to survive. The temperature on the surface of Venus is 462°C – that's **hot enough to melt lead!** And if that is not bad enough, the atmosphere is so acidic, it would eat through your space suit, and so thick and heavy it would **crush your body to pulp!**

The planets Jupiter, Saturn, Uranus and Neptune are giant balls of cold gas. They do not have oceans or land where life could live. Pluto is rocky, but because it is so far from the Sun, it is so cold that even air would freeze solid. Nothing could survive there …

Freaky Fact

I like to be different!

All the planets in our solar system rotate anticlockwise, except Venus. It is the only planet that rotates clockwise.

But there is at least one other place in the solar system where conditions may be suitable for life. Orbiting the planet Jupiter is the mysterious moon, Europa. Europa is about the same size as our Moon, but unlike the Moon, its surface is not rock but ice. Scientists believe that underneath the ice there are oceans of liquid water. Europa is kept warm enough for the water to stay liquid by the force of gravity working on it, as it spins in its orbit close to the giant planet, Jupiter.

QUIZ The Sun is not a planet. It is a ****.

Perhaps there is life in the oceans of Europa. There are plans to send a robot probe to drill through the ice to find out!

We have not yet discovered life anywhere else than on Earth. But the search has only just begun! Finding living things that have not developed on Earth would be one of the most amazing discoveries **EVER!** It would mean that we are not alone in the universe … Perhaps, somewhere on a planet similar to Earth, orbiting a star like the Sun, there are other intelligent creatures that we might one day communicate with!

ET Phone Home

Heat and light from the Sun make life on Earth possible. But the Sun is not special. There are billions of stars in the universe just like the Sun. Scientists have discovered that other stars have planets orbiting them in just the same way that Earth orbits the Sun. Are they inhabited too? If there are other inhabited planets out there, why haven't aliens visited Earth? One reason may be that stars are so far apart that even at the **speed of light** (the fastest speed that anything can travel) it would take many years to make the journey from one star to another.

The Sun is our star!

43

But if it is too far to travel, perhaps we, like ET, could talk on the telephone! Scientists are already using radio telescopes to search the skies for signals that could come from extraterrestrial life. If you have a PC at home, you can take part in this search yourself – read on to find out how!

The Arecibo radio telescope is a huge dish more than three times the size of a football pitch. It picks up faint radio signals that are created naturally by the movements of stars and galaxies as they spin, explode, collapse and collide. They sound like the hiss on your radio when it is not tuned in properly.

If intelligent extraterrestrials are transmitting signals, these would stand out as regular bleeps against background hiss.

Scientists from the Search for Extraterrestrial Intelligence (SETI) project are searching through the radio signals from the Arecibo telescope for regular radio pulses that might come from another planet. If you have a PC connected to the Internet, you can take part in the search yourself by logging onto:

`http://setiathome.ssl.berkeley.edu/index.html`

QUIZ Radio signals from outer space are transmitte

FiNDiNG aLiENS FaCT

If the SETI project succeeds, the intelligent extraterrestrials discovered may not be anything like us, or even the aliens we imagine in films. Their bodies might be made from computer microchips, or clouds of gas floating in space – we just don't know!

Who knows, perhaps you will be the first person to discover life in space ...

******** by stars and galaxies moving.

Now that we are back on the solid ground of planet Earth, did you get all these answers to the quiz questions? Juggle with the first letters of all six answers to make an out-of-this-world word mentioned in this book.

- International
- Expedition
- Apollo
- Star
- Laika
- Naturally

Juggle with the first letters LAIESN and you get ALIENS – greetings earthlings!